D1551263

Pp

Bela Davis

Abdo
THE ALPHABET
Kids

abdopublishing.com

Published by Abdo Kids, a division of ABDO, PO Box 398166, Minneapolis, Minnesota 55439.
Copyright © 2017 by Abdo Consulting Group, Inc. International copyrights reserved in all countries.
No part of this book may be reproduced in any form without written permission from the publisher.

Printed in the United States of America, North Mankato, Minnesota.

102016

012017

THIS BOOK CONTAINS
RECYCLED MATERIALS

Photo Credits: Glow Images, iStock, Shutterstock

Production Contributors: Teddy Borth, Jennie Forsberg, Grace Hansen

Design Contributors: Christina Doffing, Candice Keimig, Dorothy Toth

Publisher's Cataloging in Publication Data

Names: Davis, Bela, author.

Title: Pp / by Bela Davis.

Description: Minneapolis, Minnesota : Abdo Kids, 2017 | Series: The alphabet |
    Includes bibliographical references and index.

Identifiers: LCCN 2016943896 | ISBN 9781680808926 (lib. bdg.) |
    ISBN 9781680796025 (ebook) | ISBN 9781680796698 (Read-to-me ebook)

Subjects: LCSH: English language--Alphabet--Juvenile literature. | Alphabet
    books--Juvenile literature.

Classification: DDC 421/.1--dc23

LC record available at http://lccn.loc.gov/2016943896

Table of Contents

Pp

Pi**p**er **p**aints a **p**icture.

4

Pp

Paris makes a**pp**le **p**ie.

Pp

Paige goes to a **p**izza **p**arty.

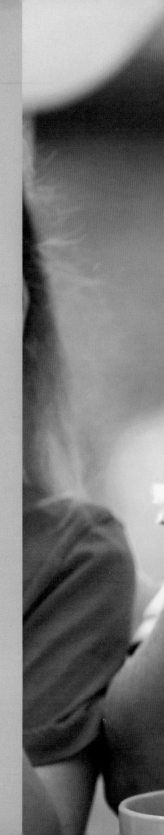

8

Pp

Pedro **performs** in the **p**lay.

11

Pp

Pat sni**p**s **p**ink **p**a**p**er.

13

Pp

Parker is **proud** to be in the **p**arade.

Pp

Peyton hel**p**s **p**ick **p**eaches.

16

Pp

Paul wears a **p**ur**p**le to**p**.

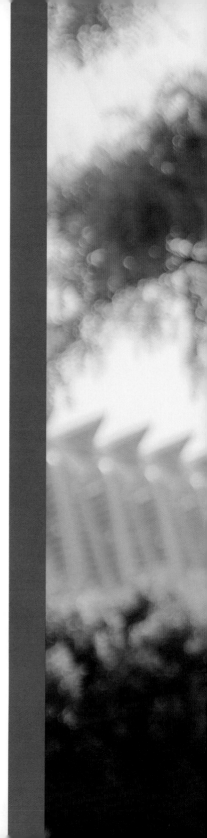

Pp

What does **P**ete **p**lay?

(**p**iano)

More Pp Words

panda

pirate

penny

popcorn

Glossary

perform
to entertain an audience by singing, acting, etc.

proud
very happy and pleased of something you have done.

Index

abdokids.com

Use this code to log on to abdokids.com and access crafts, games, videos, and more!

Abdo Kids Code:
TPK8926